POCKET-SIZED TECHNOLOGY

GADGETS THAT FIT IN YOUR POCKETS!

TECHNOLOGY BOOK FOR KIDS
CHILDREN'S INVENTORS BOOKS

In this book, we're going to talk about high-tech gadgets that fit in your pockets. So, let's get right to it!

New high-tech gadgets are coming out every year. Some of them are improved versions of products that have been around for quite some time and others are completely new.

FITNESS BRACELET

Zip Activity Tracker

The Fitbit Company makes many high-tech gadgets to help people track their exercise activity. One of their newest products is called a Zip Activity Tracker. This tiny, high-tech device clips onto your workout clothes and tracks your physical activity in detail.

It tracks every step you take, computes the distance, and gives you a summary of the calories you burned when exercising. It then sends the data to your online account.

It helps you set your fitness goals by providing you with graphs to show your progress and badges when you reach important milestones.

MINI DIGITAL CAMERA

Mini Digital Toy Camera

Lots of different high-tech gadgets take photos, but if you want an inexpensive camera that's almost a disposable, then the Chobi Cam Toy Camera might be just the right gadget for you. It only weighs about 16 grams and is smaller than the palm of your hand.

It looks like a yellow wedge of Swiss cheese. It can take high-resolution still photos. It can also record your voice and 45 minutes of video. It has a micro SD (secure digital) card that has 32 gigabytes of memory, so it's pretty powerful for a tiny toy. Next time you give someone the direction "Say Cheese" you can do it with a cheese camera!

CHEESE TOY CAMERA

IPOD CLASSIC

iPod

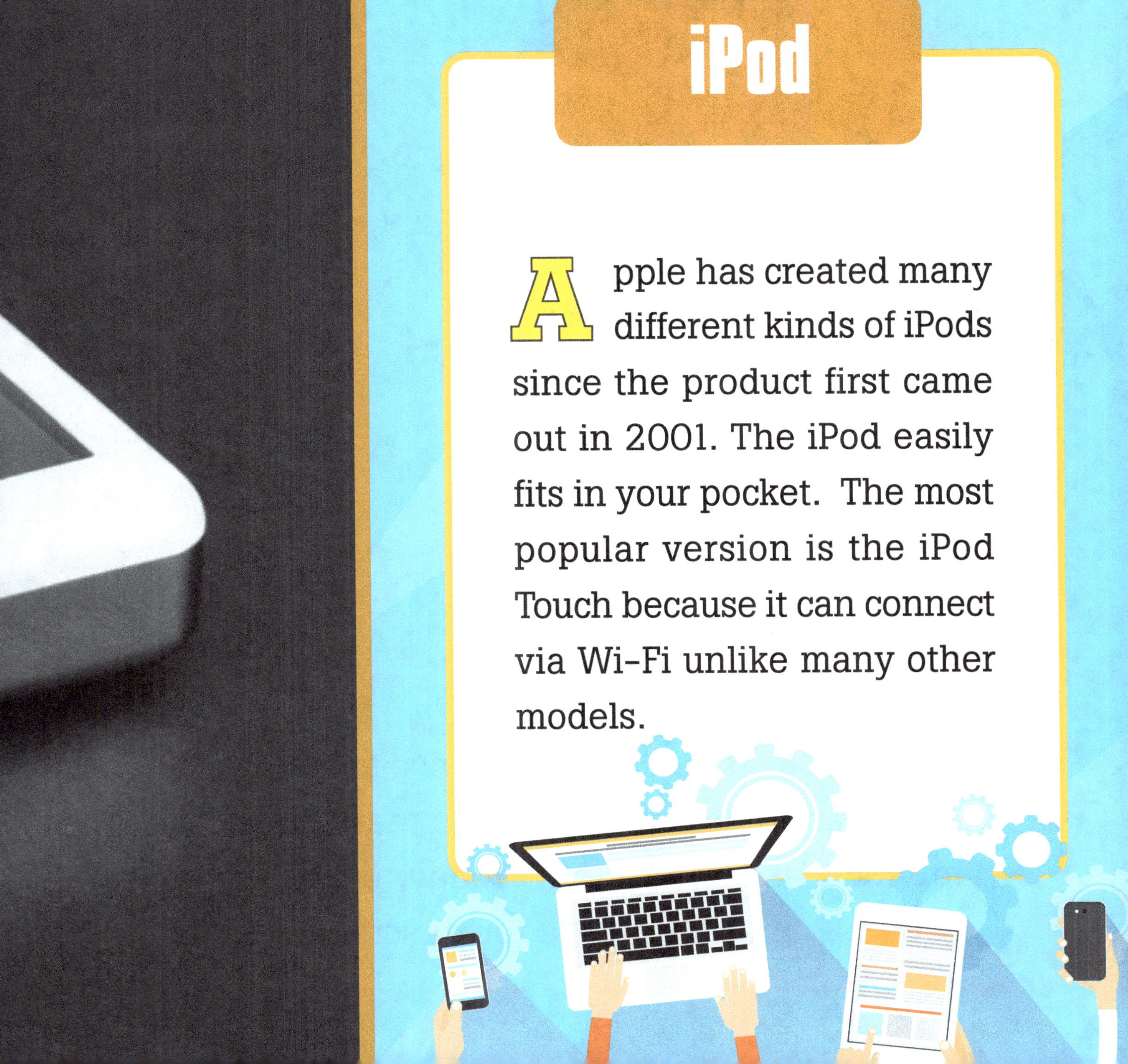

A pple has created many different kinds of iPods since the product first came out in 2001. The iPod easily fits in your pocket. The most popular version is the iPod Touch because it can connect via Wi-Fi unlike many other models.

The iPod started out as a device to listen to a library of a thousand songs that you could download and store to it. Today, it has those features, but it also has a touch screen like an

iPhone. In addition to using it to access your music, you can take photos and videos with it. You can create a movie trailer with it by using iMovie.

LISTENING TO MUSIC ON AN IPOD

Because iPod Touch can connect to the cloud via Wi-Fi, you can tap into an unlimited source of storage for photos and videos using iCloud. It can connect to iTunes Match, which is Apple's cloud service for storing your music collection, and also to iTunes Radio, which is an Apple radio service that streams on the internet. You can watch movies and play games or access educational apps on the iPod Touch too.

The iPod Touch also has Siri, which is a personal assistant in the form of a voice. Siri is a type of artificial intelligence. She speaks many different languages. You can ask Siri questions and she will answer. Kids who don't even know how to type words yet can get Siri to help them send messages on the iPod Touch using iMessage.

83%
04:12
Song 04
0:12
3:21

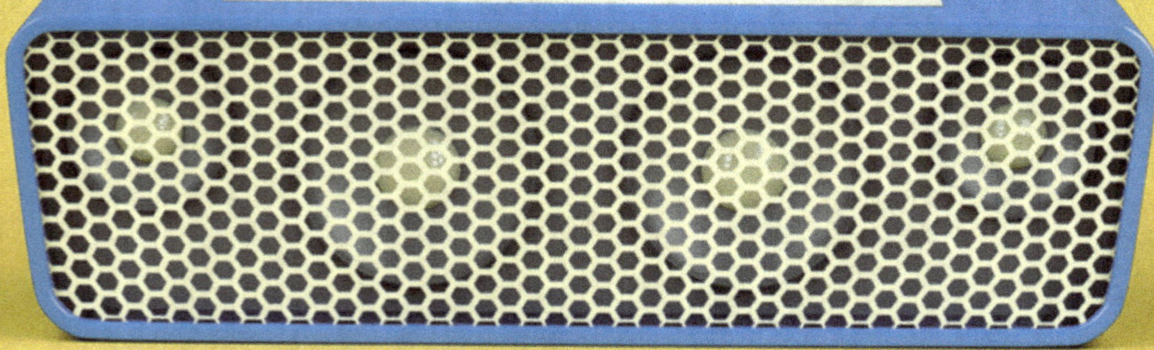

SPEAKER DOCK

There are lots of different speakers that are built to connect to the iPod. Because the iPod is a small device, when it plays music or podcasts it can use speakers to amplify the sound.

There are some speakers that are too big to fit in your pocket, but there is a special speaker dock that looks something like a Lego block.

It's very tiny and comes in lots of different colors. It's a fun way to get better sound from your iPod.

Smartphone

There are many different types of smart phones on the market. Smartphones are coming out with new features every year. You can make calls and send texts on your smartphone. You can also access the internet, your email, and your social media accounts.

SMARTPHONES

CHECKING THE WEATHER WITH A SMARTPHONE IS POSSIBLE

You can get the weather report, take photos and videos, play games, and read a map all on your smartphone. Some even have built-in projectors to project an image at a larger size. In the not-so-distant future, smartphones may even be able to project holograms, which are three-dimensional images formed with light beams!

Smartstick

There's only one problem with smartphones. They run out of power. When you're at home, you can hook them up to a power outlet and recharge them. However, sometimes they run out of power when you're out and about.

MOBILE PHONE WITH RED POWER BANK

The smartstick made by a company called "Pebble" is a pocket-sized battery charger for your smartphone and other handheld devices.

It's so powerful that it can give your phone a full charge.

Mini LED Bed Lamp

If you like to read or study while you're propped up in bed, then you may want to get a mini bed lamp. This tiny LED lamp has a clamp to attach it to different bed designs. All you need are the batteries for it and it will illuminate your reading area without casting light all over the room. It's also a great lamp for when you are traveling.

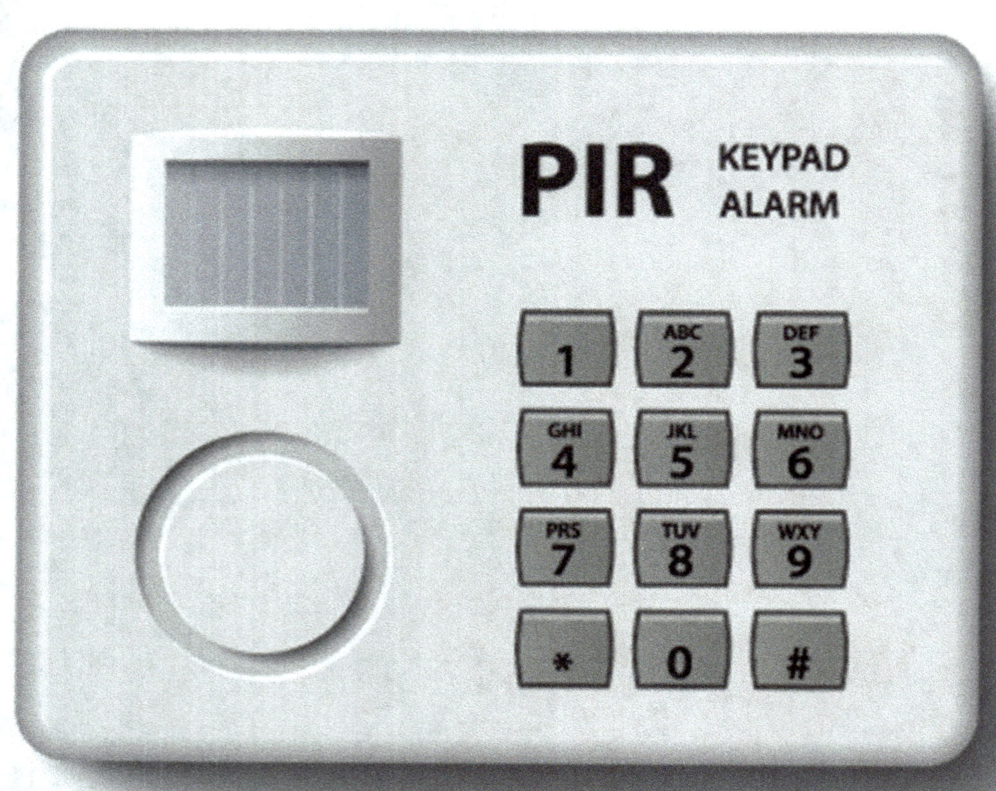

MOTION DETECTOR KEYPAD INFRARED ALARM

Motion Sensitive Alarm

When you're traveling sometimes it's good to have extra protection. There are small, pocket-sized, high-tech alarms on the market that you can attach to a door or window.

MOTION DETECTOR INFRARED ALARM

Not too much bigger than a thumbnail drive, they detect motion and set off a loud alarm if anyone tries to enter your room.

They can also be used on public bathroom stalls that don't have proper locks. These alarms ensure that you are safe and have privacy.

Mini Drone

A mini drone is one of the most fun tech gadgets on the planet. These pocket-sized flying machines can be used both indoors and out for hours of flying fun. The remote control used to operate your drone is pocket-sized too.

The smallest drone on the market is only a little over 1 inch square, but it can do all sorts of sophisticated flying maneuvers including forward and backward flips and barrel rolls. It even stabilizes itself if it's tossed into the air.

TRACKING DEVICES

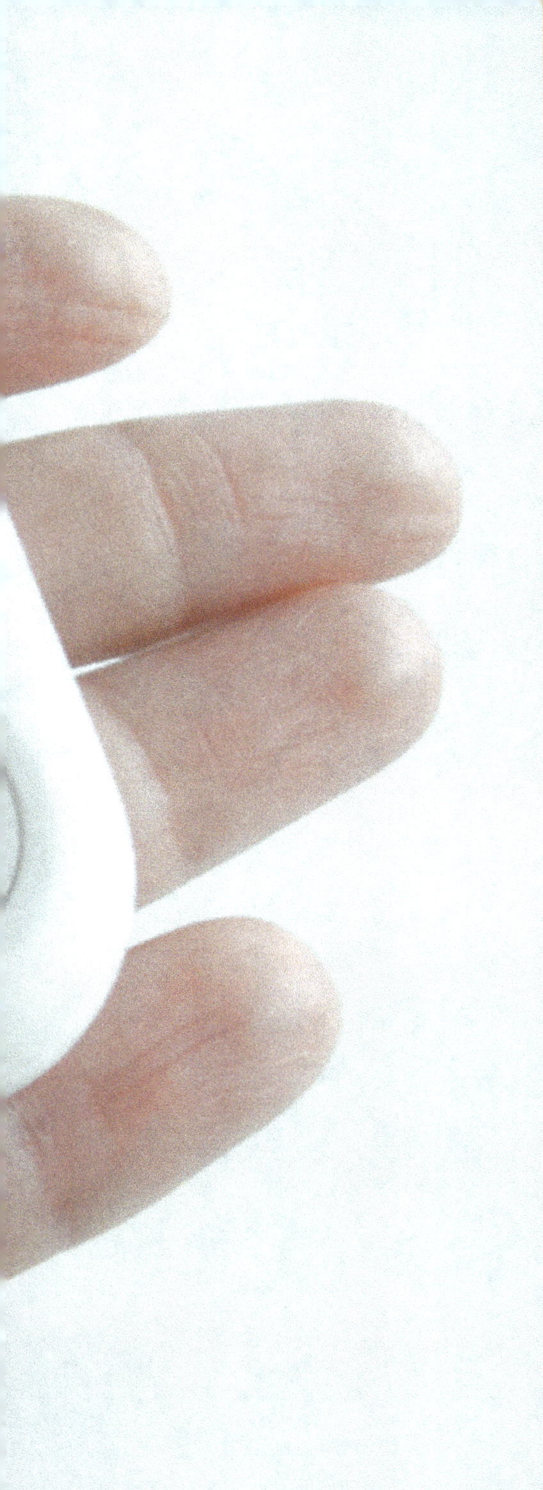

Coin-Sized Tracking Device

Are you in the habit of losing things? Then, you might want the new pocket-sized tracking device that's shaped like a coin. All you have to do is attach the tracking device to your valuable item, such as your keys, your phone, or your wallet.

You can use the device to ring your phone even if you put your phone into silent mode. You can use the software app that accompanies the tracking device to alert other users to help you find your item too. You can even attach the device to your pet.

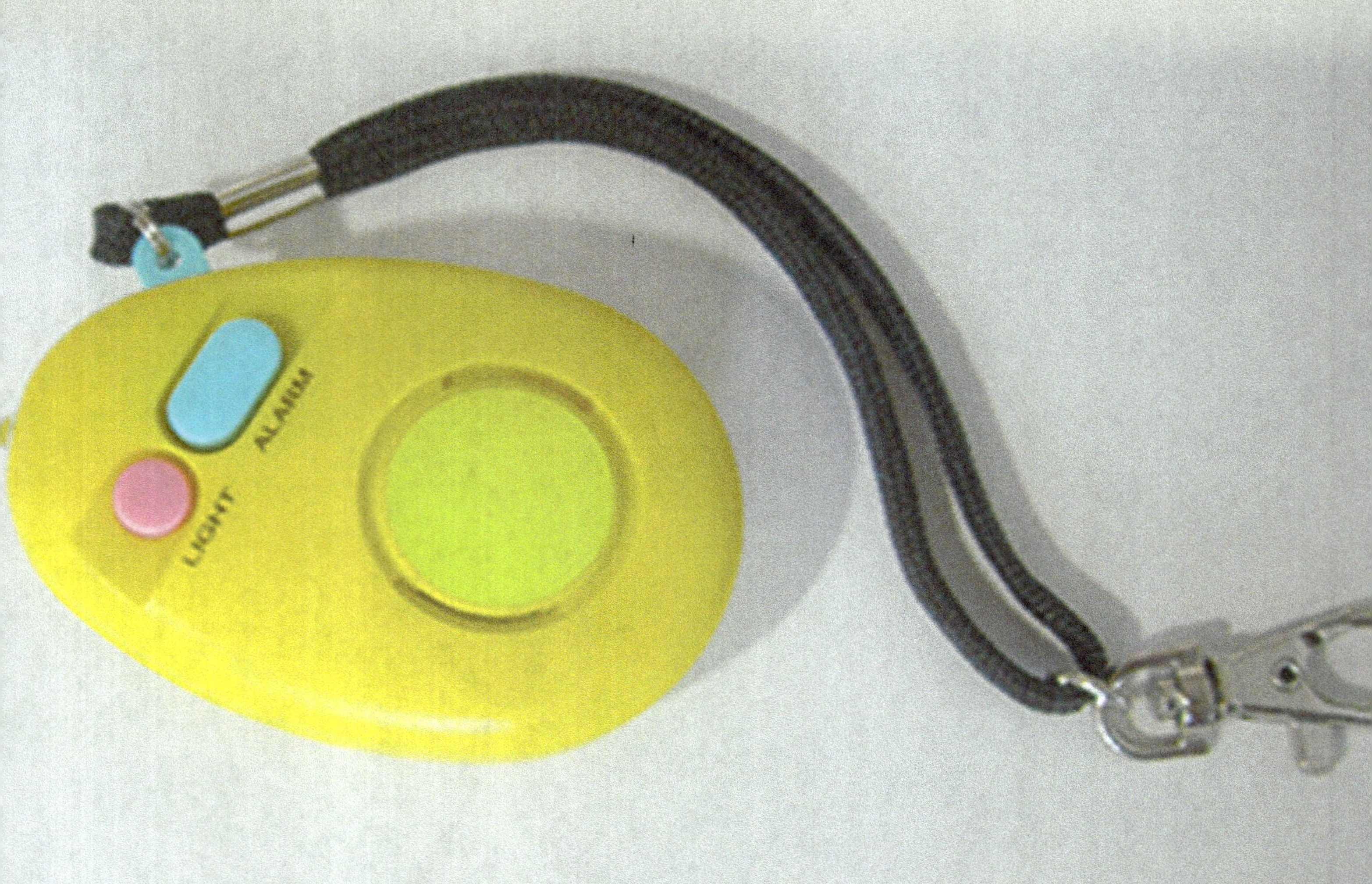
ALARM
LIGHT

Siren Song Protection Device

This pocket-sized, egg-shaped, high-tech device attaches to your keychain or other item you carry with you all the time. If you feel that you are in danger, you can sound the alarm, which emits a 130-decibel sound that is deafening, but very effective in getting attention for help. This device is also good for people who have health problems and can't call out for help.

High-Tech Wallet

Did you know that criminals are able to scan your credit cards from a regular wallet? Once your cards are scanned they can use them to buy things or steal your identity. However, there are now sleek, high–tech wallets made out of thin metal or other material that prevents criminals from scanning your credit cards.

GPS Wristband

Parents always worry about their children. One device that helps give them peace of mind is a GPS wristband. Some of these high-tech wristbands double as watches also. The GPS (global positioning system) allows parents to know exactly where a child is at any time. These types of devices are also helpful for people who have memory loss. They may get lost and not know where they are and by using the GPS, their caregivers can find them.

Handheld Game Device

Many manufacturers have different handheld devices specifically for playing video games. Some of them contain over 200 games so whenever you want to do something fun, you can just take the device out of your pocket and start playing.

MULTIMEDIA VIDEO OR COMPUTER GAMES

SUMMARY

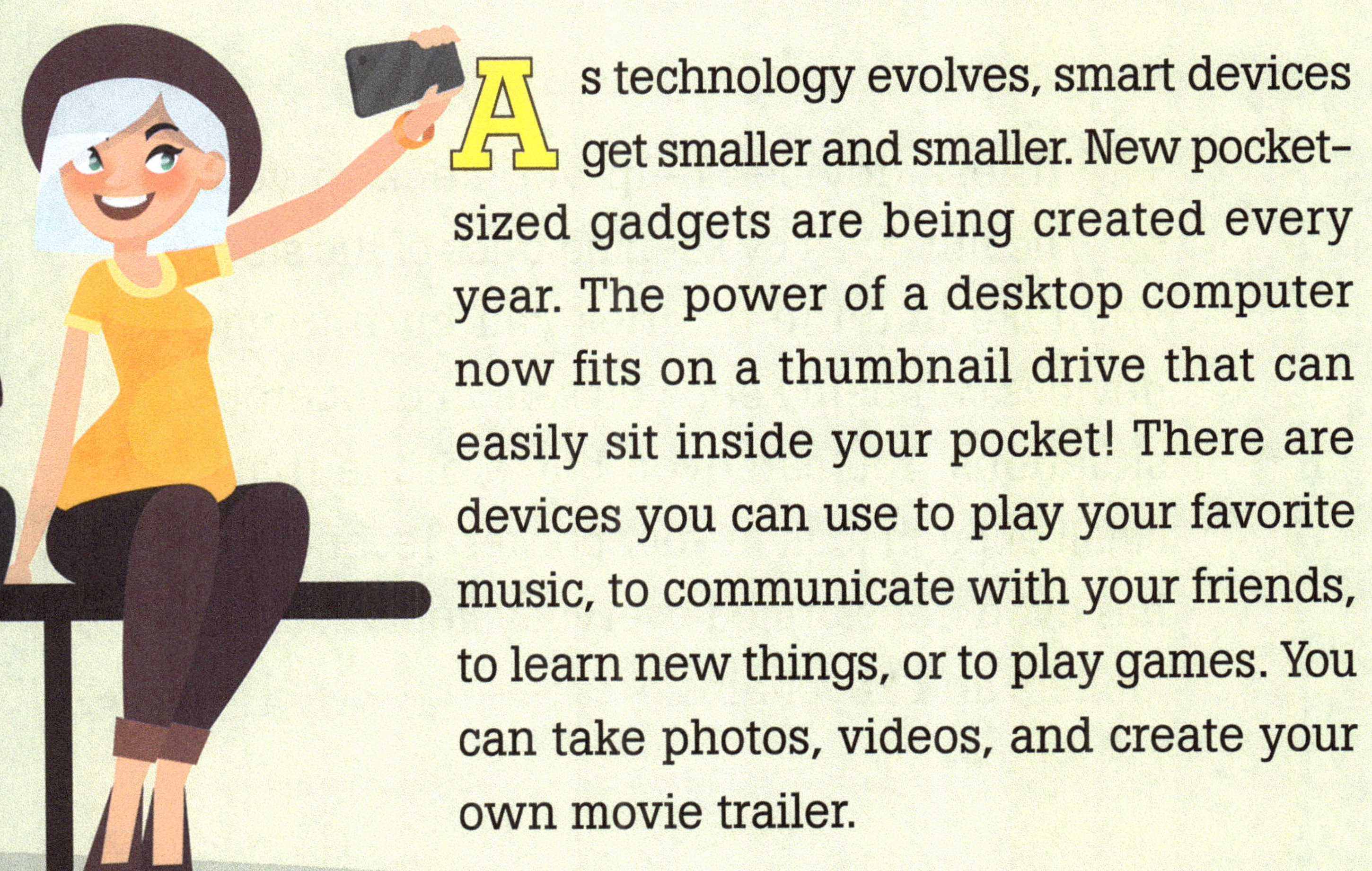

As technology evolves, smart devices get smaller and smaller. New pocket-sized gadgets are being created every year. The power of a desktop computer now fits on a thumbnail drive that can easily sit inside your pocket! There are devices you can use to play your favorite music, to communicate with your friends, to learn new things, or to play games. You can take photos, videos, and create your own movie trailer.

Fitness devices help you stick to your health goals by keeping track of the steps you take and the calories you burn. Some devices can help keep you safe in dangerous situations. You can even buy a drone that's small enough to fit in your pocket. Technology has even transformed everyday items such as wallets and keychains.

EXCERCISING WHILE LISTENING TO MUSIC

Awesome! Now that you've read about high-tech gadgets that fit in your pockets, you may want to read about cell phones in the Baby Professor book

From Cell Phones to VOIP: The Evolution of Communication Technology - Technology Books.

Visit
BABY PROFESSOR
EDUCATION KIDS
www.BabyProfessorBooks.com
to download Free Baby Professor eBooks
and view our catalog of new and exciting
Children's Books